Delicious Keto Desserts.

Best 50, Tasty, Low Carb Recipes for Weight loss and Healthy Life.

Table of Contents

Introduction

What is the Ketogenic Diet?

Rising use of the ketogenic diet by people from all around the world makes us think about the significance and outcomes of this carb-limited diet plan. How can complete aversion from carbohydrates, a macronutrient, lead to better health? The idea is simple. In the absence of these carbs and in the presence of a large number of fats, our body can work to produce energy through the process of ketosis instead of breaking down sugar molecules. Ketosis is the metabolic activity in which fat molecules are broken down to produce large packets of energy and ketone molecules. The science behind the ketogenic diet is therefore directly related to ketosis. Normally when we intake an unlimited amount of carbohydrates, they have the tendency to deposit themselves in the body and do not allow the fats to be consumed. But of course, we cannot completely avoid carbs in our diet as they are present in every other food ingredient. What we can do is set a limit on its consumption. The ketogenic diet does that for you. It says to keep the carb intake under 10 to 12 grams per meal, whereas a good intake of fats is encouraged.

Important Facts about Ketosis

To understand ketosis more deeply and to sum it all up, let's go through some important facts about ketosis:

- Ketosis only occurs in the complete absence of glucose.
- It is a process in which stored fats are actively broken down into released energy and ketones as a by-product.
- Keeping a balanced approach while following a ketogenic plan is of utmost important, as it can also cause ketosis, which leads to ketoacidosis, and it can be fatal.
- People with type 1 diabetes are more prone to develop ketoacidosis. Therefore it is not suggested to type 1 patients. Every person wishing to attempt the diet should contact an expert first.

The History of Ketogenic Diet

The rise of the ketogenic diet dates back to the 1920s to 1930s as a food therapy for epilepsy, a brain-related disease. Unlike other medicated treatments, the ketogenic diet worked due to its long-lasting impact. It emerged as a good alternative to fasting, which was previously used to treat epilepsy. But the idea of keto therapy soon faced a failure due to lack of research and extensive use of medications.

However, in 1921, Rollin Woodyatt revived the idea of ketogenic dieting and brought its benefits back into the spotlight when he spotted the three important compounds being produced in the bodies of those who either fasted or ate a low carb and high-fat diet. Soon Russel Wilder termed such a diet as "Ketogenic" due to its known effects of producing a high number of ketones in the body. From that point on, the concept of Ketosis prevailed. However, it did not gain widespread public attention until 1997 when Charlie Abraham's epilepsy was treated through the use of a complete Ketogenic Diet plan. The scientific community and ordinary individuals both showed interest in the study of the ketogenic diet, rising over the next ten years. By 2007, the idea had spread to up to 45 countries around the world. People actively sought this diet plan, not only to treat specific diseases, but also to reduce weight and avoid cardiovascular disease.

Levels of Ketogenic Diet:

To help understand the effects of the ketogenic diet and the steady change towards adopting its new food style, experts have divided the entire cycle into three major phases: the induction phase, adjustment phase, and fitness phase. These phases chalk out a complete roadmap to a fully-fledged keto routine.

1. Induction Phase:

Entering into the world of the ketogenic diet requires more of the mental strength than physical. It is important to prepare your mind for it and then act on it. Thus, the first phase is all about preparing yourself for this special diet. An easy way to do that is by removing all the possible high-carb food items from your groceries and opting for more clean carbs. Do your research and plan things out for yourself. Be steadier and more gradual to have a more lasting impact. Start limiting the number of carbs and keep track of the fats intake. Habit and discipline are crucial while surviving through this phase. Loss of will means loss of efforts, so start sticking to the routine.

2. Adjustment Phase:

Now that the induction phase has passed, the adjustment phase allows a person to add more variety to the diet using a variety of keto-friendly fruits and vegetables. It is safe to add more fats to the diet through creams, cheeses or vegetable oils. In this phase, the body goes through slight changes in terms of energy levels and health. This adjustment in the diet is important to keep up with the pace of those changes.

3: Fitness Phase:

The last phase of this process is the fitness phase. By this time, the routine for the keto diet must be well developed. However, the body still needs a kick-start to burn more fat than glucose. A little exercise is recommended at this stage to help achieve this goal. Such exercise may range from light aerobics to high-intensity exercises. Physical exercises paired with a planned ketogenic diet are the road to a healthy and active life.

Benefits of Ketogenic Diet:

1. Fat Burn

The main objective of a keto diet is to consume fats as a source of energy instead of carbohydrates. Therefore, when a person is on a keto diet, more fats present in the body are burned, which consequently reduces weight and prevents obesity.

2. Lower Cholesterol:

Consumption of fats in the energy-producing process means reduced cholesterol levels in the blood. This is particularly important for patients suffering from cardiovascular diseases and higher cholesterol levels.

3. Lower Blood Sugar:

Diabetes, or a high blood sugar level, is caused due to zero or minimum production of the insulin hormone in the body. People suffering from such a disorder cannot regulate their blood sugar levels naturally. Therefore, they need a diet low on sugars, and the ketogenic diet is the best option for such individuals.

4. Increased Energy:

A single fats molecule can produce three times more energy than a carbohydrate when broken down. This is the reason why the use of the ketogenic diet gives us an instant and long-lasting boost of energy after a meal.

5. Vitality:

Though scientists are still trying to bring out direct evidence of the effects of the ketogenic diet on the increased vitality of a person, they have concluded that keto food improves health in the longer run, aides an active metabolism and detoxifies the body regularly, which all can lead to increased vitality.

6. Mental focus:

While it is true that the ketogenic diet originally came to use for the treatment of mental illnesses like epilepsy and Alzheimer's, it is also true that a lower consumption of carbohydrates and higher availability of ketones in the body detoxify the blood and nourish neural cells.

7. Reduce obesity:

There is a huge misconception that an intake of more fats can cause obesity. It is true when you take fats along with excessive carbohydrates. Fats like those in the keto diet do not cause obesity. Instead, the fats reduce obesity by consuming all the deposited fats in the body.

8. Metabolism:

Increased energy production through ketosis leads to a better metabolism. Due to the presence of fat molecules in the food, the body works rigorously during and after the digestion to generate energy.

What to Eat on a Ketogenic Diet?

To make things simple and easier, let's break it down a little and try to understand the Keto vegetarian diet plan as a chart explaining what to have and what not to have. Down below is a brief list of all the items which can be used on a Ketogenic vegetarian diet.

- **Meats**

All types of meat are free from carbohydrates, so it is always safe to use meat in the ketogenic diet. However, processed meat, which may contain high traces of carbohydrates, should be avoided.

- **Keto Friendly Vegetables**

Keep in mind that not all vegetables are low on carbs. There are some that are full of starch, and they need to be avoided. A simple technique to assess the suitability of the vegetables for a keto diet is to check if they are 'grown above the ground' or 'below it.' All vegetables which are grown underground are a no-go for Keto, whereas vegetables which are grown above are best for keto and these mainly include cauliflower, broccoli, zucchini, etc. Among the vegetables, all the leafy green vegetables can be added to this diet, including spinach, kale, parsley, cilantro, etc.

- **Seeds and Dry Nuts**

Nuts and seeds like sunflower seeds, pistachios, pumpkin seeds, almonds, etc. can all be used on a ketogenic diet.

- **Dairy Products**

Not every dairy product is allowed on a keto diet. For example, milk is a no-go for keto, whereas hard cheeses, high fat cream, butter, eggs, etc. can all be used.

- **Fruits:**

Not all berries are Keto friendly; only choose blackberries or raspberries, and other low-carb berries. Similarly, not all fruits can be taken on a keto diet; avocado, coconut, etc. are keto friendly, whereas orange, apple, and pineapple, etc. are high in carbohydrates.

- **Fats:**

Ghee, butter, plant oils, and animal fats are all forms of fats can be used on a ketogenic diet.

- **Ketogenic Sweeteners:**

As sugar is strictly forbidden for a ketogenic diet, may it be brown or white, there are certain substitutes which can be used like stevia, erythritol, monk fruit, and other low-carb sweeteners.

Table: Food to Eat

Meat	Vegetables	Fruits	Nuts	Oils	Dairy
Beef	Artichoke hearts	Avocados	Almonds	Almond oil	Coconut milk
Chicken	Arugula	Blueberries	Brazil nuts	Avocado oil	Almond milk
Pork	Asparagus	Coconuts	Hazelnuts/filberts	Cacao butter	Coconut cream
Fish	Bell peppers	Cranberries	Macadamia nuts	Coconut oil	butter
Turkey	Beets	Lemons	Pecans	Flaxseed oil	Cheeses
Duck	Bok choy	Limes	Peanuts	Hazelnut oil	Silken Tofu
Quail	Broccoli	Olives	Pine nuts	Macadamia nut oil	ghee
Shrimp	Brussels sprouts	Raspberries	Walnuts	MCT oil	
Lobsters	Cabbage	Strawberries	Chia	Olive oil	
Mussels	Carrots	Tomatoes	Hemp	Healthy oils	
Prawns	Cauliflower	Watermelon	Pumpkin	Almond oil	
	Celery				

What to Avoid?

Avoiding carbohydrates is the main aim of a ketogenic diet. Most of the daily items we use contain a high amount of carbohydrates in the form of sugars or starches. In fact, any amount of these items drastically increase the carbohydrate value of your meal. So, it is best to avoid their use completely.

1. Grains:

All types of grains are high in carbohydrates, whether its rice or corn or wheat. Any product extracted from them is equally high in carbs, like cornflour, wheat flour or rice flour. So, while you need to avoid these grains for keto, their flours should also be avoided. Coconut and almond flours can be used as a good substitute.

2. Legumes:

Legumes are also the underground parts of the plants; thus, they are rich in carbohydrates. Make no mistake of using them in your diet. These include all sorts of beans, from Lima to chickpeas, Garbanzo, black, white, red beans, etc. Cross all of them off your grocery list if you are about to go keto. All types of lentils are also not allowed on a keto diet.

3. Sugar:

Besides white and brown sugar, there are other forms of it which are also not keto friendly, and this list includes honey, agave, molasses, maple syrup, etc. Also, avoid chocolates, which are high in sugar. Use special sweeteners and sugar-free chocolates only.

4. Fruits:

Certain fruits need to be avoided while on a keto diet. Apples, bananas, oranges, pineapples, etc. all fall into that category. Do not use them in any form. Avoid using their flesh, juice, and mash to keep your meal carb free.

5. Tubers:

Tubers are basically the underground vegetables, and some of them are rich in carbs, including potatoes, yams, sweet potatoes, beets, etc.

6. Dairy:

As stated above, not all dairy products can be freely used on a ketogenic diet. Animal milk should be strictly avoided.

Table: Food Not to Eat

Sugars	Fruits	Grains	Legumes	Tubers	Dairy
White	Apples	Rice	Lentils	Yams	Animal milk
brown	Banana	Wheat	Chickpeas	Potatoes	
Maple syrup	Pineapples	Corn	Black beans	Beets	
Agave	Oranges	Barley	Garbanzo beans		
Honey, Molasses	Pears	Millet	Lima Beans		
Confectioner's sugar	Pomegranate	Oats	Kidney beans		
Granulated sugar	Watermelon	Quinoa	White beans		

Mistakes while Following a Ketogenic Diet:

Though the diet lays out a simple eating plan for each consumer, it can still be overwhelming for beginners. It takes time to get acquainted with all the Dos and Don'ts of the plan. The following mistakes are, however, quite common and should be avoided.

1. Substitution

For Keto users, conversion from simpler sugars to artificial sugars like stevia and others is not easy at first. Many people substitute the amount as it is, which later spoils the entire recipe. Always keep in mind to use the sweeteners as per your taste.

2. Use of milk

As most of the other animal products are allowed on the ketogenic diet, many people assume that milk is also keto friendly and continue its intake. It is not true though, as milk is a high-carb product and should be substituted with coconut or almond milk.

3. Not everything natural is Keto friendly

Many people believe that sugars present in fruits are not harmful enough to disrupt your ketogenic diet routine, which is not true at all. Fruits like apples, pineapple, etc. are high in carbs and hence strictly forbidden. The same thing goes for a number of vegetables.

4. Irregularity

To notice the results of a ketogenic diet, a person needs to be patient and persistent. Many people do not follow a routine, which is a must for a keto diet.

5. Not consulting a doctor

Before setting off on this venture, it is always suggested to get yourself medically checked and start the diet only when your physician gives you the OK.

6. Sudden shift

Most people switch to the keto diet too suddenly, which sometimes results in complexities and a number of difficulties. It is always recommended to be gradual while opting for this diet plan.

Conclusion:

The entire length of this comprehensive ketogenic diet book gives its reader a brief and precise overview of the term ketogenic, its origin, its various phases, the benefits of the diet, and the use of the keto friendly food items and related recipes. Give your body a break and let it harness energy through the invigorating process of ketosis. Read this ketogenic guide plan and discover ways to activate your metabolism, reduce obesity, control cholesterol and a number of other health complexities. Enjoy the best of the ketogenic dishes through quick and simple recipes.

Ketogenic Dessert Recipes

Lemony Frozen Treat

Yield: 4 servings
Preparation Time: 10 minutes

Ingredients:

- ¼ cup fresh lemon juice
- 8-ounce cream cheese softened
- 1 cup heavy cream
- 1/8 teaspoon salt
- ½ teaspoon liquid stevia

Instructions:

1. In a blender, add lemon juice and cream cheese and pulse until smooth.
2. Add remaining ingredients and pulse until well combined and fluffy.
3. Transfer the mixture into serving glasses.
4. Refrigerate to chill before serving.

Nutritional Information per Serving:

Calories: 305
Fat: 31g
Sat Fat: 9.5g
Carbohydrates: 2.7g
Fiber: 0.1g
Sugar: 0.5g
Protein: 5g
Sodium: 256mg

Frozen Vanilla Yogurt

Yield: 6 servings
Preparation Time: 15 minutes

Ingredients:

- 3 cups plain Greek yogurt
- 3-4 drops liquid stevia
- 1 teaspoon organic vanilla extract
- ¼ cup fresh strawberries, hulled and sliced

Instructions:

1. In a bowl, add all ingredients and mix until well combined.
2. Transfer the mixture into an ice cream maker and process according to manufacturer's directions.
3. Transfer the mixture into a bowl and freeze, covered for about 30-40 minutes or until desired consistency.
4. Garnish with strawberry slices and serve

Nutritional Information per Serving:

Calories: 91
Fat: 1.5g
Sat Fat: 1.2g
Carbohydrates: 9g
Fiber: 0.1g
Sugar: 9g
Protein: 7g
Sodium: 86mg

Frozen Avocado Yogurt

Yield: 6 servings
Preparation Time: 15 minutes

Ingredients:

- 1 avocado, peeled, pitted and chopped roughly
- 1 (15-ounce) can coconut cream
- 1 cup plain Greek yogurt
- 2 tablespoons fresh lime juice
- 1 teaspoon liquid stevia

Instructions:

1. In a food processor, put all ingredients and pulse until smooth.
2. Transfer the mixture into an airtight container and freeze for about 6 hours, stirring after every 45 minutes.
3. Remove from freezer and set aside at room temperature for about 10-15 minutes before serving.

Nutritional Information per Serving:

Calories: 261
Fat: 23.9g
Sat Fat: 16.8g
Carbohydrates: 9g
Fiber: 3.8g
Sugar: 5.4g
Protein: 4.6g
Sodium: 41mg

Pecan Ice Cream

Yield: 6 servings
Preparation Time: 15 minutes
Cooking Time: 5 minutes

Ingredients:

- 2 tablespoons butter
- 1 cup heavy cream
- 1/3 cup Erythritol
- Dash of liquid stevia
- 2 organic egg yolks
- 1 teaspoon organic vanilla extract
- 2/3 cup pecans, chopped
- 1/8 teaspoon xanthan gum

Instructions:

1. In a pan, add butter over low heat and cook until browned slightly, stirring frequently.
2. In the pan, place the cream and bring to a slow boil.
3. Reduce the heat to very low.
4. Add Erythritol and mix until dissolved completely.
5. Remove the pan from heat and place the cream mixture into a bowl.
6. Add the stevia and mix until well combined.
7. With an electric hand mixer, blend until well combined.
8. Slowly, add the xanthan gum, beating at medium speed until well combined.
9. In a small bowl, place the egg yolks and vanilla extract and beat until well combined.
10. Add the egg yolk mixture into cream mixture and beat until well combined.
11. Gently, fold in the pecans and xanthan gum.
12. Place the mixture into ice cream-maker and process according to manufacturer's directions.
13. Now, place into an airtight container and place in the freezer overnight before serving.

Nutritional Information per Serving:

Calories: 224
Fat: 22.9g
Sat Fat: 8.6g
Carbohydrates: 3.4g
Fiber: 2.1g
Sugar: 0.7g
Protein: 2.9g
Sodium: 49mg

Cheesecake Ice Cream

Yield: 7 servings
Preparation Time: 15 minutes
Cooking Time: 7-8 minutes

Ingredients:

- ½ cup Erythritol
- 3 organic egg yolks
- 1½ cups heavy cream
- 1 cup unsweetened almond milk
- 4-ounce cream cheese softened
- ½ teaspoon xanthan gum
- ½ teaspoon organic vanilla extract
- ½ teaspoon monk fruit liquid extract

- ¼ teaspoon liquid stevia
- 1 cup fresh raspberries
- 1 packet powdered stevia

Instructions:

1. In a bowl, add Erythritol and egg yolks and beat until well combined. Set aside.
2. In a medium pan, add cream and almond milk and bring to boil.
3. Slowly, add hot cream mixture into egg yolk mixture, beating continuously until well combined.
4. In the same pan, add the mixture over medium heat and cook until mixture becomes thick, stirring continuously.
5. Remove from the heat and place the remaining ingredients except for raspberries and stevia packet, beating continuously until smooth.
6. Transfer the mixture into a bowl.
7. Arrange the bowl into an ice bath to cool completely.
8. Transfer the mixture into an ice cream maker and process according to manufacturer's directions.
9. In a bowl, add raspberries and stevia packet and with a fork, mash well.
10. In an airtight container, place half of ice cream mixture and top with half of the mashed raspberries.
11. With a wooden skewer, swirl the mixture.
12. Repeat with the remaining ice cream mixture and mashed raspberries.
13. Freeze for about 2 hours before serving.

Nutritional Information per Serving:

Calories: 422
Fat: 43.1g
Sat Fat: 26g
Carbohydrates: 6g
Fiber: 1.5g
Sugar: 1g
Protein: 4.7g
Sodium: 114mg

Spinach Sorbet

Yield: 4 servings
Preparation Time: 15 minutes

Ingredients:

- 3 cups fresh spinach, chopped
- 1 tablespoon fresh basil leaves
- ½ of an avocado, peeled, pitted and chopped
- ¾ cup unsweetened almond milk
- 18-20 drops liquid stevia
- 1 teaspoon almonds, chopped very finely
- 1 teaspoon organic vanilla extract
- 1 cup ice cubes

Instructions:

1. In a food processor, put all ingredients and pulse until smooth.
2. Transfer into an ice cream maker and process according to manufacturer's directions.
3. Now, place into an airtight container and freeze for at least 4-5 hours before serving.

Nutritional Information per Serving:

Calories: 70
Fat: 5.9g
Sat Fat: 1.1g
Carbohydrates: 3.6g
Fiber: 2.4g
Sugar: 0.4g
Protein: 1.4g
Sodium: 53mg

Strawberry Sorbet

Yield: 4 servings
Preparation Time: 15 minutes

Ingredients:

- 2½ cups fresh strawberries, hulled and halved
- 1/3 cup Erythritol
- 1/3 cup unsweetened almond milk
- 1 tablespoon fresh lemon juice
- 1 teaspoon liquid stevia
- ¼ teaspoon salt

Instructions:

1. In a food processor, put all ingredients and pulse until smooth.
2. Transfer into an ice cream maker and process according to manufacturer's directions.
3. Now, place into an airtight container and freeze for at least 4-5 hours before serving.

Nutritional Information per Serving:

Calories: 33
Fat: 0.6g
Sat Fat: 0.1g
Carbohydrates: 7.2g
Fiber: 1.9g
Sugar: 4.5g
Protein: 0.7g
Sodium: 164mg

Coffee Granita

Yield: 8 servings
Preparation Time: 15 minutes

Ingredients:

- 4 cups hot brewed extra strong coffee
- 2 teaspoons ground cinnamon
- ½ cup Erythritol
- 1¼ cups heavy cream, divided

Instructions:

1. In a large bowl, add coffee, cinnamon, and Erythritol and stir until dissolved completely.
2. Add ¼ cup of cream and beat until well combined.
3. Refrigerate for about 30 minutes.
4. Remove from refrigerator and transfer the mixture into a shallow baking dish.
5. Freeze for about 3 hours, scraping after every 30 minutes with the help of a fork.

6. Just before serving, in a bowl, add remaining cream and beat until soft peaks form.
7. Place the granita into serving glasses and top each with whipped cream.
8. Serve immediately.

Nutritional Information per Serving:

Calories: 67
Fat: 7g
Sat Fat: 4.3g
Carbohydrates: 1g
Fiber: 0.3g
Sugar: 0g
Protein: 0.5g
Sodium: 10mg

Lemon Granita

Yield: 8 servings
Preparation Time: 15 minutes

Ingredients:

- 3 cups water
- 2 cups fresh lemon juice
- ½ cup powdered Erythritol
- 1 teaspoon fresh lemon zest, grated
- 5-10 fresh mint leaves
- Pinch of sea salt

Instructions:

1. In a food processor, put all ingredients and pulse until smooth.
2. Through a fine mesh sieve, strain the mixture into a baking dish, discarding the pulp.
3. Refrigerate for about 30 minutes.

4. Remove from refrigerator and scrape the mixture well.
5. Freeze for about 3 hours, scraping after every 30 minutes with the help of a fork.
6. Just before serving, scrape the granita well.
7. For a very smooth, scrape more with a fork, or place in a food processor and pulse until it resembles smooth snow.

Nutritional Information per Serving:

Calories: 15
Fat: 0.5g
Sat Fat: 0.5g
Carbohydrates: 1.4g
Fiber: 0.3g
Sugar: 1.3g
Protein: 0.5g
Sodium: 46mg

Berry Popsicles

Yield: 6 servings
Preparation Time: 15 minutes

Ingredients:

- 5-ounce cream cheese softened
- ¼ cup full-fat coconut milk
- 3 tablespoons plain yogurt
- ¼ cup powdered Erythritol
- 2 tablespoons coconut, shredded
- 1 teaspoon chia seeds
- ½ teaspoon MCT oil
- 1/3 cup frozen blueberries
- 1/3 cup frozen raspberries

Instructions:

1. In a food processor, put all the ingredients excluding berries and pulse until smooth.
2. Add the berries and pulse until chopped into small pieces.
3. Transfer the mixture into popsicle molds.
4. Insert 1 popsicle stick in each mold and freeze for about 3-4 hours or until set.

Nutritional Information per Serving:

Calories: 140
Fat: 11.9g
Sat Fat: 8.3g
Carbohydrates: 6.9g
Fiber: 1.3g
Sugar: 4.8g
Protein: 2.8g
Sodium: 77mg

Chocolate Popsicles

Yield: 10 servings
Preparation Time: 15 minutes
Cooking Time: 5 minutes

Ingredients:

- 2½-ounce 70% chocolate, chopped finely
- 2 large organic eggs
- 1¾ cups heavy cream
- 1/3 cup Erythritol
- ¾ cup unsweetened almond milk
- 1 teaspoon organic vanilla extract

Instructions:

1. In a large pan, add chocolate, eggs, cream and, Erythritol over medium-low heat and cook until just boiling, beating continuously.
2. Immediately, remove from the heat.

3. In the pan, place the almond milk and vanilla extract and stir to combine well.
4. Transfer the mixture into popsicle molds.
5. Insert 1 popsicle stick in each mold and freeze for about 5 hours or until set.

Nutritional Information per Serving:

Calories: 129
Fat: 11.1g
Sat Fat: 6.6g
Carbohydrates: 5.1g
Fiber: 0.3g
Sugar: 3.8g
Protein: 2.3g
Sodium: 41mg

Cheesecake Mousse

Yield: 6 servings
Preparation Time: 15 minutes

Ingredients:

- 1 (8-ounce) package cream cheese, softened
- 1/3 cup powdered Erythritol
- 1/8 teaspoon liquid stevia
- 1½ teaspoons organic vanilla extract
- ¼ teaspoon lemon extract
- 1 cup heavy whipping cream
- ½ teaspoon fresh lime zest, grated

Instructions:

1. In a bowl, add cream cheese and beat until smooth.
2. Add the Erythritol, stevia and both extracts and beat until well combined.

3. In another bowl, add heavy cream and with an electric mixer, beat until stiff peaks form.
4. Add ½ of the whipped cream into the cream cheese mixture and gently, stir to combine.
5. Now, fold in remaining whipped cream.
6. Now, with an electric beater, beat on high speed until light and fluffy.
7. Refrigerate for about 2-3 hours.
8. Transfer the mixture into serving glasses and serve with the garnishing lime zest.

Nutritional Information per Serving:

Calories: 204
Fat: 20.6g
Sat Fat: 12.9g
Carbohydrates: 1.7g
Fiber: 0g
Sugar: 0.2g
Protein: 3.3g
Sodium: 120mg

Chocolate Mousse

Yield: 2 servings
Preparation Time: 10 minutes

Ingredients:

- 2½ cups water, divided
- 1 cup ricotta cheese
- 2 teaspoons powdered stevia
- 2 teaspoons cacao powder
- ½ teaspoon organic vanilla extract
- 2 tablespoons fresh raspberries

Instructions:

1. In a large bowl, place all the ingredients except raspberries and beat until well combined.
2. Transfer the mousse into 2 serving glasses and refrigerate to chill for about 4-6 hours or until set completely.
3. Serve with the garnishing of raspberries.

Nutritional Information per Serving:

Calories: 182
Fat: 10.2g
Sat Fat: 6.3g
Carbohydrates: 8.3g
Fiber: 1g
Sugar: 0.9g
Protein: 14.5g
Sodium: 155mg

Strawberry Fluff

Yield: 6 servings
Preparation Time: 15 minutes

Ingredients:

- 1½ cups heavy cream
- 1 (8-ounce) package cream cheese, softened
- 1 cup fresh strawberries, hulled and halved
- ½ teaspoon liquid stevia
- ¼ teaspoon monk fruit extract
- 1 teaspoon unflavored gelatin
- 2 tablespoons boiling water
- ¼ cup fresh strawberries, hulled and chopped
- 1 tablespoon fresh mint leaves

Instructions:

1. In a large bowl, add cream, cream cheese, halved strawberries, stevia, and monk fruit extract and beat until well combined.
2. In another bowl, add the gelatin and boiling water and stir until well combined.
3. Slowly, add gelatin mixture into strawberry mixture, beating continuously until well combined.
4. Transfer the mixture into serving bowls and refrigerate for about 3-4 hours.
5. Serve with the garnishing of chopped strawberries and mint leaves.

Nutritional Information per Serving:

Calories: 247
Fat: 24.4g
Sat Fat: 15.2g
Carbohydrates: 4.2g
Fiber: 0.7g
Sugar: 1.6g
Protein: 4g
Sodium: 125mg

Cheese Pudding

Yield: 6 servings
Preparation Time: 15 minutes
Cooking Time: 35 minutes

Ingredients:

- 1 cup cottage cheese
- ¾ cup heavy cream
- 3 organic eggs
- ¾ cup water
- ½ cup Erythritol
- 1 teaspoon organic vanilla extract
- ¼ teaspoon ground cinnamon

Instructions:

1. Preheat oven to 350 degrees F.
2. Generously, grease 6 (6-oz.) ramekins.
3. In a blender, add all ingredients except cinnamon and pulse until smooth.
4. Transfer the mixture into prepared ramekins evenly and sprinkle each with cinnamon.
5. In a large baking dish, place the ramekins
6. Add hot water in the baking dish, about 1-inch up sides of the ramekins.
7. Place the baking dish in oven and bake for about 35 minutes.
8. You can serve this pudding warm and chilled as well.

Nutritional Information per Serving:

Calories: 119
Fat: 8.5g
Sat Fat: 4.6g
Carbohydrates: 2.1g
Fiber: 0.1g
Sugar: 0.4g
Protein: 8.3g
Sodium: 190mg

Vanilla Pudding

Yield: 5 servings
Preparation Time: 15 minutes
Cooking Time: 3 minutes

Ingredients:

- 1 tablespoon powdered stevia
- 1/8 teaspoon xanthan gum
- 3 organic egg whites
- 1 cup heavy cream
- ½ cup unsweetened coconut milk
- 1 teaspoon organic vanilla extract
- 2 tablespoons fresh blueberries

Directions:

1. In a large bowl, mix together stevia and xanthan gum.
2. Add remaining ingredients except blueberries and with an electric mixer, beat on high speed for about 3 minutes.
3. Transfer the mixture into a heavy-bottomed pan over medium-high heat and cook for about 3 minutes, stirring continuously.
4. Now, place the mixture into a bowl and set aside to cool completely.
5. Refrigerate for about 1 hour.
6. Garnish with blueberries and serve.

Nutritional Information per Serving:

Calories: 153
Fat: 14.6g
Sat Fat: 10.6g
Carbohydrates: 2.9g
Fiber: 0.7g
Sugar: 1.4g
Protein: 3.2g
Sodium: 34mg

Pumpkin Custard

Yield: 6 servings
Preparation Time: 10 minutes
Cooking Time: 50 minutes

Ingredients:

For Custard:

- 1 (15-ounce) can pumpkin puree
- 4 organic eggs, beaten
- ½ cup heavy cream
- 2 teaspoons vanilla extract
- 1 teaspoon cinnamon liquid stevia
- 2 teaspoons pumpkin pie spice
- ¼ teaspoon salt

For Topping:

- 1/3 cup whipped cream
- 1/8 teaspoon ground cinnamon

Instructions:

1. Preheat the oven to 350 degrees F.
2. Grease 6 ramekins.
3. For custard: in a large bowl, add all ingredients and beat until smooth.
4. Transfer the mixture into prepared ramekins evenly.
5. Bake for about 45-50 minutes.
6. Remove from oven and place the ramekins onto a wire rack to cool slightly.
7. Top each ramekin with whipped cream evenly.
8. Sprinkle with cinnamon and serve.

Nutritional Information per Serving:

Calories: 126
Fat: 9g
Sat Fat: 4.6g
Carbohydrates: 7.1g
Fiber: 2.2g
Sugar: 2.8g
Protein: 4.9g
Sodium: 148mg

Coffee Custard

Yield: 4 servings
Preparation Time: 15 minutes
Cooking Time: 8 minutes

Ingredients:

- ¼ cup unsalted butter
- 4-ounces mascarpone cheese
- 4 large organic eggs (whites and yolks separated)
- 1 teaspoon espresso powder
- 1 tablespoon water
- ¼ teaspoon cream of tartar
- ¼ teaspoon monk fruit extract drops
- ½ teaspoon liquid stevia

Instructions:

1. In a medium pan, add butter and cream cheese over medium-low heat and cook, for about 2-3 minutes or until melted completely, stirring continuously.
2. Add egg yolks, espresso powder, and water and stir to combine.
3. Set the heat to low and cook, uncovered for about 2-4 minutes or until desired thickness, stirring continuously.
4. Meanwhile, in a bowl, add cream of tartar and egg whites and beat until stiff peaks form.
5. Remove from the heat and stir in fruit extract drops and stevia.
6. Gently, fold in egg white mixture.
7. Transfer into serving glasses and refrigerate to chill before serving.

Nutritional Information per Serving:

Calories: 224
Fat: 20.2g
Sat Fat: 11.2g
Carbohydrates: 1.5g
Fiber: 0g
Sugar: 0.5g
Protein: 9.6g
Sodium: 176mg

Creamy Flan

Yield: 6 servings
Preparation Time: 15 minutes
Cooking Time: 1 hour 10 minutes

Ingredients:

- 1 cup Erythritol, divided
- 1 cup plus 1 tablespoon water, divided
- 5 organic eggs
- 1/8 teaspoon salt
- 1¾ cups heavy cream
- 1 teaspoon organic vanilla extract

Instructions:

1. Preheat the oven to 325 degrees F.

2. For caramel: in a small pan, add ½ cup of Erythritol and 1 tablespoon of water over medium-low heat and cook until sweetener is melted completely, stirring continuously.
3. Remove from the heat and place the caramel in the bottom of a round baking dish evenly.
4. Set aside for about 10 minutes.
5. In a bowl, add the remaining Erythritol, eggs, and salt and beat until well combined. Set aside.
6. In a medium pan, add remaining water and cream and bring to a boil.
7. Remove from the heat.
8. Slowly, add hot cream mixture into egg yolk mixture, beating continuously until well combined.
9. Add the mixture into the pan with the remaining cream mixture and mix well.
10. Now, place the vanilla extract and mix well.
11. Place the cream mixture over the caramel in the baking dish evenly.
12. Arrange the baking dish in a large roasting pan.
13. Add hot water in the roasting pan about 1-inch up sides of the baking dish.
14. Place the roasting pan in oven and bake for about 55-60 minutes or until center becomes set.
15. Remove from oven and place the baking dish onto a wire rack to cool for about 1 hour.
16. Refrigerate to chill completely before serving.

Nutritional Information per Serving:

Calories: 175
Fat: 16.6g
Sat Fat: 9.2g
Carbohydrates: 1.4g
Fiber: 0g
Sugar: 0.4g
Protein: 5.3g
Sodium: 115mg

Cream Cheese Flan

Yield: 10 servings
Preparation Time: 15 minutes
Cooking Time: 1 hour 5 minutes

Ingredients:

- ¾ cup Erythritol, divided
- 3 tablespoons water, divided
- 2 teaspoons organic vanilla extract, divided
- 5 large organic eggs
- 2 cups heavy whipping cream
- 8-ounce full-fat cream cheese softened
- ¼ teaspoon sea salt

Instructions:

1. Preheat the oven to 350 degrees F.
2. Grease an 8-inch cake pan.
3. For caramel: in a heavy-bottomed pan, add ½ cup of Erythritol, 2 tablespoons of water and 1 teaspoon of vanilla extract over medium-low heat and cook until sweetener is melted completely, stirring continuously.
4. Remove from the heat, and place the caramel in the bottom of the prepared cake pan evenly.
5. In a blender, add remaining Erythritol, vanilla extract, heavy cream, cream cheese, eggs, and salt and pulse until smooth.
6. Place the cream mixture over caramel evenly.
7. Arrange the cake pan in a large roasting pan.
8. Add hot water in the roasting pan about 1-inch up sides of the cake pan.
9. Place the roasting pan in oven and bake for about 1 hour or until center becomes set.
10. Remove from oven and place the cake pan in a water bath to cool completely.
11. Refrigerate for about 4-5 hours before serving.

Nutritional Information per Serving:

Calories: 200
Fat: 19.3g
Sat Fat: 11.3g
Carbohydrates: 1.6g
Fiber: 0g
Sugar: 0.4g
Protein: 5.4g
Sodium: 158mg

Vanilla Crème Brûlée

Yield: 4 servings
Preparation Time: 15 minutes
Cooking Time: 1 hour

Ingredients:

- 2 cups heavy cream
- 1 vanilla bean, halved and scraped out seeds
- 4 organic egg yolks
- 1/3 teaspoon stevia powder
- 1 teaspoon organic vanilla extract
- Pinch of salt
- 4 tablespoons Erythritol

Instructions:

1. Preheat the oven to 350 degrees F.
2. In a pan, add heavy cream over medium heat and cook until heated.

3. Stir in vanilla bean seeds and bring to a gentle boil.
4. Reduce the heat to very low and simmer, covered for about 20 minutes.
5. Meanwhile, in a bowl, add remaining ingredients except for Erythritol and beat until thick and pale mixture forms.
6. Remove the heavy cream from heat and through a fine mesh sieve, strain into a bowl.
7. Slowly, add cream in egg yolk mixture beating continuously.
8. Transfer the mixture into 4 ramekins evenly.
9. Arrange the ramekins into a large baking dish.
10. Add hot water in the baking dish, about half of the ramekins.
11. Bake for about 30-35 minutes.
12. Remove from oven and transfer the ramekins into a refrigerator for at least 4 hours.
13. Just before serving, sprinkle the ramekins with Erythritol evenly.
14. Holding a kitchen torch about 4-5-inches from the top, caramelize the Erythritol for about 2 minutes.
15. Set aside for about 5 minutes before serving.

Nutritional Information per Serving:

Calories: 264
Fat: 26.7g
Sat Fat: 15.4g
Carbohydrates: 2.4g
Fiber: 0g
Sugar: 0.3g
Protein: 3.9g
Sodium: 31mg

Pumpkin Crème Brûlée

Yield: 8 servings
Preparation Time: 15 minutes
Cooking Time: 45 minutes

Ingredients:

- 3 tablespoons powdered Erythritol
- 4 large organic egg yolks
- 1 cup heavy cream
- ½ cup unsweetened almond milk
- ½ cup homemade pumpkin puree
- ½ teaspoon organic vanilla extract
- ½ teaspoon pumpkin pie spice
- ¼ teaspoon salt
- 4 teaspoons granulated Erythritol

Instructions:

1. Preheat the oven to 300 degrees F.
2. Arrange 8 crème brûlée ramekin dishes in a large baking dish.
3. In a bowl, add powdered Erythritol and egg yolks and beat until slightly thick mixture forms. Set aside.
4. In a small pan, add cream and almond milk over medium-high heat and cook until just beginning to bubble, stirring frequently.
5. Remove from heat.
6. Slowly, add egg mixture into cream mixture, beating continuously until well combined.
7. Add pumpkin puree, vanilla extract, pumpkin pie spice, and salt and beat until well combined.
8. Transfer the mixture into the ramekins about ¾ full.
9. Add cold water in the baking dish, about half of the ramekins.
10. Bake for about 30-40 minutes.
11. Remove from oven and transfer the ramekins into a refrigerator for at least 4 hours.
12. Just before serving, sprinkle the ramekins with granulated Erythritol evenly.
13. Holding a kitchen torch about 4-5-inches from the top, caramelize the Erythritol for about 2 minutes.
14. Set the ramekins aside for about 8-10 minutes before serving.

Nutritional Information per Serving:

Calories: 88
Fat: 8.1g
Sat Fat: 4.3g
Carbohydrates: 2.2g
Fiber: 0.5g
Sugar: 0.6g
Protein: 1.9g
Sodium: 96mg

Vanilla Panna Cotta

Yield: 4 servings
Preparation Time: 15 minutes
Cooking Time: 5 minutes

Ingredients:

- 2 teaspoons unflavored powdered gelatin
- 2 tablespoons water
- 2 cups heavy whipping cream
- 1 tablespoon organic vanilla extract
- 2 tablespoons fresh blueberries
- 8 fresh mint leaves

Instructions:

1. In a bowl, add the gelatin and water and mix until well combined. Set aside.
2. In a pan, add cream and vanilla extract and bring to a boil.
3. Set the heat to medium-low and simmer for about 2 minutes.

4. Remove the pan of cream from heat and mix in the gelatin mixture until well combined.
5. Transfer the mixture into serving glasses evenly and set aside to cool completely.
6. With plastic wrap, cover each glass and refrigerate for about 4-5 hours.
7. Remove the glasses from a refrigerator and set aside at room temperature for about 30 minutes before serving.
8. Serve with the garnishing of blueberries and mint leaves.

Nutritional Information per Serving:

Calories: 223
Fat: 22.2g
Sat Fat: 13.8g
Carbohydrates: 2.8g
Fiber: 0.1g
Sugar: 0.9g
Protein: 2.3g
Sodium: 27mg

Chocolate Panna Cotta

Yield: 4 servings
Preparation Time: 15 minutes
Cooking Time: 5 minutes

Ingredients:

- 1½ cups unsweetened almond milk, divided
- 1 tablespoon unflavored powdered gelatin
- 1 cup unsweetened coconut milk
- 1/3 cup Swerve
- 3 tablespoons cacao powder
- 2 teaspoon instant coffee granules
- 6 drops liquid stevia
- 3 tablespoons mixed berries

Instructions:

1. In a large bowl, add ½ cup of almond milk and sprinkle with gelatin evenly. set aside until soaked.
2. In a pan, add remaining almond milk, coconut milk, almond milk, Swerve, cacao powder, coffee granules and stevia and bring to a gentle boil, stirring continuously.
3. Remove from the heat.
4. In a blender, add gelatin mixture and hot milk mixture and pulse until smooth.
5. Transfer the mixture into serving glasses evenly and set aside to cool completely.
6. With plastic wrap, cover each glass and refrigerate for about 3-4 hours.
7. Serve with the garnishing of berries.

Nutritional Information per Serving:

Calories: 177
Fat: 16.4g
Sat Fat: 13.3g
Carbohydrates: 6.9g
Fiber: 3.1g
Sugar: 2.5g
Protein: 5.3g
Sodium: 80mg

Raspberry Soufflé

Yield: 6 servings
Preparation Time: 15 minutes
Cooking Time: 9 minutes

Ingredients:

- 1 cup fresh raspberries
- 5 tablespoons granulated Erythritol, divided
- 4 organic egg whites
- ½-ounce 70% dark chocolate, chopped

Instructions:

1. Preheat the oven to 400 degrees F.
2. Arrange a rack in the center of oven. Grease 6 ramekins.
3. In a blender, add raspberries and pulse until pureed.
4. Through a fine sieve, strain raspberry puree into a bowl, discarding the seeds.
5. In the bowl of raspberry puree, add 1 tablespoon of Erythritol and mix well. Set aside.
6. In a glass bowl, place egg whites and beat until thick.
7. Add remaining Erythritol and beat until stiff peaks form.
8. Gently, fold 1/3 of whipped egg whites into raspberry puree.
9. Now, fold remaining whipped egg whites into raspberry puree.
10. Place the mixture into prepared ramekins about halfway full.
11. Divide chocolate into ramekins evenly and top with remaining raspberry mixture.
12. Arrange the ramekins in a large baking sheet and bake for about 9 minutes.
13. Remove from oven and serve immediately.

Nutritional Information per Serving:

Calories: 35
Fat: 0.9g
Sat Fat: 0.5g
Carbohydrates: 4g
Fiber: 1.4g
Sugar: 2.3g
Protein: 2.8g
Sodium: 24mg

Lemon Soufflé

Yield: 4 servings
Preparation Time: 15 minutes
Cooking Time: 20 minutes

Ingredients:

- 2 large organic eggs (whites and yolks separated)
- ¼ cup Erythritol, divided
- 1 cup ricotta cheese
- 1 tablespoon fresh lemon juice
- 2 teaspoons lemon zest, grated
- 1 teaspoon poppy seeds
- 1 teaspoon organic vanilla extract

Instructions:

1. Preheat the oven to 375 degrees F.
2. Grease 4 ramekins.
3. In a clean glass bowl, add egg whites and beat until foamy.
4. Add 2 tablespoons of Erythritol and beat until stiff peaks form.
5. In another bowl, add ricotta cheese, egg yolks and remaining Erythritol and beat until well combined.
6. Now, place lemon juice and lemon zest and mix well.
7. add poppy seeds and vanilla extract and mix until well combined.
8. Add the whipped egg whites into the ricotta mixture and gently, stir to combine.
9. Place the mixture into prepared ramekins evenly.
10. Bake for about 20 minutes.
11. Remove from oven and serve immediately.

Nutritional Information per Serving:

Calories: 130
Fat: 7.7g
Sat Fat: 3.9g
Carbohydrates: 4g
Fiber: 0.2g
Sugar: 0.8g
Protein: 10.4g
Sodium: 114mg

Lemon Truffles

Yield: 15 servings
Preparation Time: 15 minutes

Ingredients:

For Truffles:

- 3-ounce Brazil nuts
- 3-ounce desiccated coconut
- 5 tablespoons fresh lemon juice
- 2 tablespoons fresh lemon zest, grated finely
- 1 tablespoon coconut butter
- 1 tablespoon xylitol
- 1 teaspoon organic vanilla extract

For Coating:

- 4 tablespoons desiccated coconut

- 1 tablespoon fresh lemon zest, grated finely

Instructions:

1. For balls: in a food processor, add all ingredients pulse until a finely crumbly mixture forms.
2. Make small equal sized balls from the mixture.
3. For coating: in a shallow dish, mix together coconut and lemon zest.
4. Coat the balls with the coconut mixture evenly.
5. Arrange the truffles onto a parchment paper lined baking sheet and refrigerate until set before serving.

Nutritional Information per Serving:

Calories: 90
Fat: 8.7g
Sat Fat: 5.2g
Carbohydrates: 3.1g
Fiber: 1.8g
Sugar: 0.9g
Protein: 1.4g
Sodium: 4mg

Raspberry Truffles

Yield: 16 servings
Preparation Time: 15 minutes

Ingredients:

- ½ cup powdered Erythritol
- 8-ounce cream cheese, softened
- 2 tablespoons heavy cream
- 3 teaspoons organic raspberry extract
- 1 teaspoon organic vanilla stevia
- Red food coloring, as required
- Pinch of salt
- ¼ cup coconut oil, melted

Instructions:

1. Line 2 baking sheets with parchment paper.
2. In a large bowl, add Swerve and cream cheese and beat until smooth.

3. Add heavy cream, raspberry extract, vanilla stevia, red food coloring, and salt and mix until well combined.
4. Gradually, add coconut oil, stirring continuously until well combined.
5. With a small scooper, place the mixture onto prepared baking sheet.
6. Place in the refrigerate for about 1-2 hours or until set completely.

Nutritional Information per Serving:

Calories: 88
Fat: 9.1g
Sat Fat: 6.5g
Carbohydrates: 0.5g
Fiber: 0g
Sugar: 0.1g
Protein: 1.1g
Sodium: 54mg

Cookie Dough Bombs

Yield: 30 servings
Preparation Time: 15 minutes

Ingredients:

- ½ cup butter softened
- 1/3 cup powdered Erythritol
- ½ teaspoon organic vanilla extract
- ½ teaspoon salt
- 2 cups almond flour
- 2/3 cup 70% dark chocolate chips

Instructions:

1. In a large bowl, place the butter and with a hand mixer, beat until light and fluffy.
2. Add Erythritol, vanilla extract and salt and beat until well combined.
3. Slowly, add flour, beating continuously until well combined.
4. Gently, fold in chocolate chips.

5. With a plastic wrap, cover the bowl and refrigerate for about 15-20 minutes before serving.
6. Make small equal sized balls from the mixture and serve.
7. Refrigerate for at least 1 hour or until set completely.

Nutritional Information per Serving:

Calories: 85
Fat: 7.3g
Sat Fat: 2.7g
Carbohydrates: 3.4g
Fiber: 0.8g
Sugar: 1.4g
Protein: 1.8g
Sodium: 63mg

Cinnamon Cookies

Yield: 15 servings
Preparation Time: 15 minutes
Cooking Time: 25 minutes

Ingredients:

- 2 cups almond meal
- 1 teaspoon ground cinnamon
- 1 organic egg
- ½ cup salted butter softened
- 1 teaspoon liquid stevia
- 1 teaspoon organic vanilla extract

Instructions:

1. Preheat the oven to 300 degrees F.
2. Grease a large cookie sheet.
3. In a large bowl, place all the ingredients and mix until well combined.
4. Make 15 equal sized balls from the mixture.
5. Place the balls in the bottom of the prepared baking sheet about 2-inch apart.
6. Bake for about 5 minutes.
7. Carefully, remove from the oven and with a fork, press down each ball.
8. Bake for about 18-20 minutes.
9. Remove from oven and place the cookie sheet onto a wire rack to cool in the pan for about 5 minutes.
10. Carefully, invert cookies onto the wire rack to cool completely before serving.

Nutritional Information per Serving:

Calories: 133
Fat: 12.8g
Sat Fat: 4.5g
Sodium: 48mg
Carbohydrates: 2.9g
Fiber: 1.7g
Sugar: 0.6g
Protein: 3.1g

Cream Cheese Cookies

Yield: 24 servings
Preparation Time: 15 minutes
Cooking Time: 15 minutes

Ingredients:

- 3 cups almond flour
- ¼ teaspoon salt
- ½ cup Erythritol
- 2-ounce cream cheese softened
- ¼ cup butter softened
- 1 large organic egg white
- 2 teaspoons organic vanilla extract

mInstructions:

1. Preheat the oven to 350 degrees F.
2. Line a larger cookie sheet with baking paper.
3. In a bowl, add flour and salt and mix well. Set aside.
4. Place the Erythritol, cream cheese and butter in the bowl of stand mixer and mix until fluffy and light.
5. Now, place the egg white and vanilla extract and mix until well combined.
6. Slowly, add flour mixture, ½ cup at a time and beat until a little crumbly dough is formed.
7. With a medium cookie scooper, place the mixture onto the prepared baking sheet about 1-inch apart and with your hand, flatten each ball slightly.
8. Bake for about 15 minutes.
9. Remove from oven and place the cookie sheet onto a wire rack to cool completely before serving.

Nutritional Information per Serving:

Calories: 111
Fat: 9.4g
Sat Fat: 2.2g
Carbohydrates: 3.1g
Fiber: 1.5g
Sugar: 0.1g
Protein: 3.4g
Sodium: 50mg

Meringue Cookies

Yield: 18 servings
Preparation Time: 15 minutes
Cooking Time: 40 minutes

Ingredients:

- 4 large organic egg whites
- ¼ teaspoon cream of tartar
- 6 tablespoons powdered Swerve, divided
- 1/3 teaspoon almond extract
- Pinch of salt

Instructions:

1. Preheat the oven to 210 degrees F. Line 2-3 baking sheets with parchment papers.
2. In a bowl, add egg whites and the cream of tartar and with an electric mixer, beat on medium speed until frothy.
3. Add 3 tablespoons of Swerve, almond extract, and salt and beat on high speed until the egg whites are whipped into a medium consistency.
4. Add remaining Swerve and beat on a high speed until very stiff.
5. Scrape the meringue and beat until well combined.
6. Transfer the meringue into a piping bag, fitted with a large star-shaped tip and pipe rosette shape cookies onto the prepared baking sheets.
7. Bake for about 40 minutes.
8. Turn the oven off but keep the baking sheets in the oven for about 1 hour with a little door opened.
9. Remove from oven and put the cookie sheet onto a wire rack for about 30 minutes before serving.

Nutritional Information per Serving:

Calories: 6
Fat: 0g
Sat Fat: 0g
Carbohydrates: 0.8g
Fiber: 0g
Sugar: 0.1g
Protein: 0.8g
Sodium: 15mg

Chocolate Biscotti

Yield: 8 servings
Preparation Time: 15 minutes
Cooking Time: 30 minutes

Ingredients:

- 2 cups whole almonds
- 2 tablespoons chia seeds
- 1 organic egg
- ¼ cup coconut oil
- ¼ cup unsweetened coconut, shredded
- ¼ cup cacao powder
- 1 teaspoon baking soda
- 1/3 teaspoon powdered stevia
- ¼ teaspoon salt

Instructions:

1. Preheat the oven to 350 degrees F.
2. Line a baking sheet with parchment paper.
3. In a food processor, add almonds and chia seeds and pulse until fine.
4. Add remaining ingredients and pulse until a dough forms.
5. Transfer the dough onto a piece of foil and shape into a log.
6. Refrigerate the dough log for about 30 minutes.
7. Carefully, cut the dough log into 8 biscotti-shaped slices.
8. Bake for about 12 minutes.
9. Remove from oven and put the baking sheet onto a wire rack to cool slightly before serving.
10. Serve warm.

Nutritional Information per Serving:

Calories: 237
Fat: 21.7g
Sat Fat: 8g
Carbohydrates: 8.5g
Fiber: 5.5g
Sugar: 1.2g
Protein: 7.1g
Sodium: 241mg

Cinnamon Donuts

Yield: 6 servings
Preparation Time: 15 minutes
Cooking Time: 28 minutes

Ingredients:

For Donuts:

- 1 cup almond flour
- 1/3 cup Erythritol
- 2 teaspoons organic baking powder
- 1 teaspoon ground cinnamon
- 1/8 teaspoon salt
- 2 large organic eggs
- ¼ cup unsweetened almond milk
- ¼ cup unsalted butter (measured solid, then melted)
- ½ teaspoon organic vanilla extract

For Coating:

- ½ cup Erythritol
- 1 teaspoon ground cinnamon
- 3 tablespoons unsalted butter (measured solid, then melted)

Instructions:

1. Preheat the oven to 350 degrees F. Generously, grease a donut pan.
2. For donut: in a large bowl, add almond flour, Erythritol, baking powder, cinnamon, and salt and mix well.
3. In another bowl, add eggs, almond milk, butter, and vanilla extract and beat until well combined.
4. Add the egg mixture into flour mixture and mix until well combined.
5. Transfer the mixture into prepared donut holes about ¾ of the way full.
6. Bake for about 22-28 minutes.
7. Remove from oven and put the donut pa onto a wire rack to cool slightly before removing from the pan.
8. Meanwhile, for coating: in a small bowl, add Erythritol and cinnamon and mix well.
9. Carefully, remove the donuts from pan and transfer onto a cutting board.
10. Coat the donuts with melted butter evenly and then, roll in the cinnamon mixture.
11. Serve.

Nutritional Information per Serving:

Calories: 261
Fat: 24.1g
Sat Fat: 9.7g
Carbohydrates: 5.7g
Fiber: 2.5g
Sugar: 0.2g
Protein: 6.3g
Sodium: 185mg

Chocolate Fudge

Yield: 24 servings
Preparation Time: 15 minutes
Cooking Time: 25 minutes

Ingredients:

- 2 cups heavy whipping cream
- 1 teaspoon organic vanilla extract
- 3-ounce butter softened
- 3-ounce 70% dark chocolate, chopped finely

Instructions:

1. In a heavy-bottomed pan, add heavy cream and vanilla and bring to a full rolling boil.
2. Set the heat to low and cook, uncovered for about 20 minutes, stirring occasionally.
3. Add butter and stir until smooth.
4. Remove the pan of cream from heat and stir in the chopped chocolate until has melted.
5. Place the mixture into a 7x7-inch baking dish evenly.
6. Refrigerate until set completely.
7. Cut into pieces and serve cold.

Nutritional Information per Serving:

Calories: 79
Fat: 7.6g
Sat Fat: 4.9g
Carbohydrates: 2.4g
Fiber: 0.1g
Sugar: 1.9g
Protein: 0.5g
Sodium: 27mg

Peanut Butter Fudge

Yield: 16 servings
Preparation Time: 15 minutes
Cooking Time: 5 minutes

Ingredients:

- 1½ cups creamy, salted peanut butter
- 1/3 cup butter
- 2/3 cup powdered Erythritol
- ¼ cup unsweetened protein powder
- 1 teaspoon organic vanilla extract

Instructions:

1. In a small pan, add peanut butter and butter over low heat and cook until melted and smooth.
2. Add Erythritol and protein powder and mix until smooth.
3. Remove from heat and stir in vanilla extract.

4. Place the fudge mixture into a baking paper lined 8x8-inch baking dish evenly and with a spatula, smooth the top surface.
5. Freeze for about 30-45 minutes or until set completely.
6. Carefully, transfer the fudge onto a cutting board with the help of the parchment paper.
7. Cut the fudge into equal sized squares and serve.

Nutritional Information per Serving:

Calories: 183
Fat: 16.1g
Sat Fat: 5g
Carbohydrates: 4.8g
Fiber: 1.4g
Sugar: 2.3g
Protein: 7.4g
Sodium: 152mg

Chocolaty Cheese Brownies

Yield: 18 servings
Preparation Time: 15 minutes
Cooking Time: 25 minutes

Ingredients:

- 5-ounce 70% dark chocolate, chopped
- 4 tablespoons butter
- 3 large organic eggs
- ½ cup Erythritol
- ¼ cup mascarpone cheese
- ¼ cup cacao powder, sifted and divided
- ½ teaspoon salt

Instructions:

1. Preheat the oven to 375 degrees F.
2. Line a 9x9-inch baking sheet with parchment.
3. In a microwave-safe bowl, add chocolate and microwave until melted completely, stirring after every 30 seconds.
4. Add butter and microwave until melted and smooth, stirring once after 10 seconds.
5. Stir well and set aside to cool slightly.
6. In a large bowl, add eggs and Erythritol and with an electric mixer, beat over high speed until frothy.
7. Add mascarpone cheese and beat on high speed until smooth.
8. Add 2 tablespoons of the cacao powder and salt and gently stir to combine.
9. Add the remaining cacao powder and stir until well combined.
10. Add the melted chocolate mixture into the egg mixture and mix until well combined.
11. Place the mixture into prepared pan evenly and with a spatula, smooth the top surface.
12. Bake for about 25 minutes.
13. Remove from oven and place the baking sheet onto a wire rack to cool completely before cutting.
14. Cut into desired sized squares and serve.

Nutritional Information per Serving:

Calories: 85
Fat: 6.4g
Sat Fat: 4g
Carbohydrates: 5.4g
Fiber: 0.6g
Sugar: 4.1g
Protein: 2.3g
Sodium: 105mg

Zucchini Brownies

Yield: 16 servings
Preparation Time: 15 minutes
Cooking Time: 25 minutes

Ingredients:

- 1¼ cups 70% dark chocolate chips
- 1/3 cup coconut oil
- ¾ cup granulated Erythritol
- ¼ cup zucchini, shredded finely and squeezed
- 2 large organic eggs
- 3 tablespoons arrowroot powder
- 2 tablespoons cacao powder

Instructions:

1. Preheat the oven to 350 degrees F.
2. Line an 8x8-inch baking dish with a lightly greased piece of foil.

3. In a microwave-safe bowl, add chocolate chips and coconut oil and microwave until melted and smooth.
4. Remove from the microwave and transfer the mixture into a large bowl.
5. Add zucchini, Erythritol and eggs and beat until well combined.
6. Add arrowroot powder and cacao powder and beat until smooth.
7. In the prepared baking dish, place the mixture evenly and with a spatula, smooth the top surface.
8. Bake for about 20-25 minutes.
9. Remove from oven and place the baking dish onto a wire rack to cool completely.
10. After cooling, cut into desired size squares and serve.

Nutritional Information per Serving:

Calories: 100
Fat: 7.8g
Sat Fat: 5.8g
Carbohydrates: 8.2g
Fiber: 0.2g
Sugar: 5.1g
Protein: 1.6g
Sodium: 9mg

Chocolate Muffins

Yield: 12 servings
Preparation Time: 15 minutes
Cooking Time: 20 minutes

Ingredients:

- 1 cup almond flour
- ½ cup Erythritol
- ½ cup cacao powder
- 1½ teaspoons organic baking powder
- ¼ teaspoon salt
- 2/3 cup heavy cream
- 3-ounce unsalted butter, melted
- 3 organic eggs
- 1 teaspoon organic vanilla extract
- ½ cup 70% dark chocolate chips

Instructions:

1. Preheat the oven to 350 degrees F.
2. Line 12 cups of a large muffin tin with paper liners.
3. In a large bowl, add flour, Erythritol, cacao powder, baking powder, and salt and mix well.
4. In another bowl, add heavy cream, butter, eggs, and vanilla extract and beat until well combined.
5. Place the egg mixture into the bowl of flour mixture and mix until just blended.
6. Gently, fold in chocolate chips.
7. Now, place the mixture into each prepared muffin cup evenly.
8. Bake for about 20 minutes or until a toothpick inserted in the center comes out clean.
9. Remove from the oven and place onto the wire rack to cool in the pan for about 5 minutes.
10. Now, invert the muffins onto the wire racks to cool before serving.

Nutritional Information per Serving:

Calories: 180
Fat: 15.8g
Sat Fat: 7.1g
Carbohydrates: 8.4g
Fiber: 2.1g
Sugar: 2.8g
Protein: 4.6g
Sodium: 115mg

Cream Pancakes

Yield: 12 servings
Preparation Time: 15 minutes
Cooking Time: 35 minutes

Ingredients:

- 1 cup almond flour
- ¼ cup coconut flour
- 1 teaspoon organic baking powder
- ¼ teaspoon salt
- ½ cup Erythritol
- ¼ cup butter, softened
- ¼ cup sour cream
- 1 teaspoon organic vanilla extract

- 4 organic eggs

Instructions:

1. Preheat the oven to 350 degrees F.
2. Line 12 cups of a large muffin tin with paper liners.
3. In a bowl, add flours, baking powder and salt and mix well.
4. In another large bowl, add Erythritol and butter and with an electric mixer, beat until fluffy and light.
5. In the bowl of butter mixture, place the sour cream and vanilla extract and beat until well blended.
6. Add 1 egg at a time and with a wire whisk, beat until well combined after each addition.
7. In the bowl of cream mixture, place flour mixture and mix until well combined.
8. Now, place the mixture into each prepared muffin cup evenly.
9. Bake for about 30-35 minutes until a wooden skewer inserted in the middle of muffins comes out clean.
10. Remove from the oven and place onto the wire rack to cool in the pan for about 5 minutes.
11. Now, invert the cupcakes onto the wire racks to cool before serving.

Nutritional Information per Serving:

Calories: 133
Fat: 11g
Sat Fat: 4g
Carbohydrates: 4.2g
Fiber: 2g
Sugar: 0.2g
Protein: 4.4g
Sodium: 104mg

Vanilla Mug Cake

Yield: 1 serving
Preparation Time: 15 minutes
Cooking Time: 1½ minutes

Ingredients:

- 2 tablespoons almond flour
- 1 tablespoon coconut flour
- 2 tablespoons Erythritol
- 1/8 teaspoon baking soda
- 1 large organic egg
- 1 tablespoon butter, melted
- ½ teaspoon organic vanilla extract
- 3-4 drops liquid stevia

Instructions:

1. In a microwave-safe mug, add flours, Erythritol, and baking soda and mix well.
2. Add remaining ingredients and with a fork, mix until well combined.
3. Microwave on High for about 70-90 seconds.
4. Remove from microwave and set aside for about 2-3 minutes before serving.

Nutritional Information per Serving:

Calories: 285
Fat: 23.3g
Sat Fat: 4.3g
Carbohydrates: 8.6g
Fiber: 4.5g
Sugar: 0.6g
Protein: 9.7g
Sodium: 307mg

Lava Cake

Yield: 2 servings
Preparation Time: 15 minutes
Cooking Time: 9 minutes

Ingredients:

- 2-ounce 70% dark chocolate
- 2-ounce unsalted butter
- 2 organic eggs
- 2 tablespoons powdered Erythritol plus more for dusting
- 1 tablespoon almond flour
- 2-4 fresh strawberries

Instructions:

1. Preheat the oven to 350 degrees F.

2. Grease 2 ramekins.
3. In a microwave-safe bowl, add chocolate, and butter and microwave on High until melted, stirring after every 30 seconds.
4. Place the eggs in a bowl and with a whisk, beat well.
5. Add the chocolate mixture, Erythritol, and almond flour and mix until well combined.
6. Divide the mixture into 2 ramekins evenly.
7. Bake for about 9 minutes until the top is set.
8. Remove from oven and set aside for about 1-2 minutes.
9. Carefully, invert the cakes onto plates and dust with extra powdered Erythritol.
10. Serve with a garnishing of the strawberries.

Nutritional Information per Serving:

Calories: 492
Fat: 44.7g
Sat Fat: 10.9g
Carbohydrates: 10g
Fiber: 4.6g
Sugar: 1.5g
Protein: 10.4g
Sodium: 73mg

Cream Cheese Cake

Yield: 12 servings
Preparation Time: 15 minutes
Cooking Time: 50 minutes

Ingredients:

- 2 cups almond flour
- 2 teaspoons organic baking powder
- ½ cup butter, chopped
- 2-ounce cream cheese softened
- 1 cup sour cream
- 1 cup Erythritol
- 1 teaspoon organic vanilla extract
- 4 large organic eggs

Instructions:

1. Preheat the oven to 350 degrees F.
2. Generously, grease a 9-inch Bundt pan.
3. In a large bowl, add almond flour and baking powder and mix well. Set aside.
4. In a microwave-safe bowl, add butter and cream cheese and microwave for about 30 seconds.
5. Remove from microwave and stir well.
6. Add sour cream, Erythritol and vanilla extract and mix until well combined.
7. Add the cream mixture into the bowl of flour mixture and mix until well combined.
8. Add eggs and mix until well combined.
9. Transfer the mixture into the prepared an evenly.
10. Bake for about 50 minutes or until a toothpick inserted in the center comes out clean.
11. Remove from oven and put onto a wire rack to cool completely before removing the pan.
12. Carefully, invert the cake from the pan.
13. Cut into desired sized slices and serve.

Nutritional Information per Serving:

Calories: 263
Fat: 23.9g
Sat Fat: 9.6g
Carbohydrates: 5.5g
Fiber: 2g
Sugar: 0.2g
Protein: 7.2g
Sodium: 109mg

Matcha Roll Cake

Yield: 10 servings
Preparation Time: 20 minutes
Cooking Time: 10 minutes

Ingredients:

For Cake:

- 1 cup almond flour
- ½ cup powdered Swerve
- ¼ cup of matcha powder
- ¼ cup psyllium husk powder
- 1 teaspoon organic baking powder
- ½ teaspoon salt
- 3 large organic eggs
- ½ cup heavy whipping cream
- 4 tablespoons butter, melted
- 1 teaspoon organic vanilla extract

For Filling:

- 3-4 tablespoons water
- 1 packet unflavored gelatin
- 2 cups heavy whipping cream
- 2 teaspoons organic vanilla extract
- ¼ cup powdered Swerve

Instructions:

1. Preheat oven to 350 degrees F.
2. Line a baking sheet with parchment paper.
3. For cake: in a bowl, add almond flour, Swerve, matcha powder, psyllium husk, baking powder and salt and mix well.
4. Now, sift the flour mixture into a second bowl.
5. In a third bowl, add remaining ingredients and beat until well combined.
6. Add the egg mixture into the bowl of flour mixture and mix until a very thick dough forms.
7. Place the dough onto prepared baking sheet and roll into an even rectangle.
8. Bake for about 10 minutes.
9. Remove from oven and put onto a wire rack to cool for about 4-5 minutes.
10. Gently, roll the warm cake with the help of parchment paper.
11. Set aside to cool completely.
12. For filling: in a microwave-safe bowl, add water and sprinkle with the gelatin. Set aside for about 5 minutes.
13. Now, microwave for about 15-20 seconds.
14. Remove from microwave and beat the gelatin mixture until smooth.
15. Place gelatin mixture and remaining ingredients in a bowl of the stand mixer and beat until cream becomes stiff.
16. Spread the whipped cream over cooled cake evenly.
17. Carefully and gently, roll the cake and freezer for about 10 minutes before slicing.
18. Cut into desired sized slices and serve.

Nutritional Information per Serving:

Calories: 247
Fat: 22.5g
Sat Fat: 10.7g
Carbohydrates: 5.9g
Fiber: 3g
Sugar: 0.3g
Protein: 5.6g
Sodium: 189mg

Simple Cheesecake

Yield: 16 servings
Preparation Time: 20 minutes
Cooking Time: 1 hour 7 minutes

Ingredients:

For Crust:

- 2 cups almond flour
- 1/3 cup butter, melted
- 3 tablespoons Erythritol
- 1 teaspoon organic vanilla extract

For Filling:

- 32-ounce cream cheese softened
- 1¼ cups powdered Erythritol
- 3 large organic eggs

- 1 tablespoon fresh lemon juice
- 1 teaspoon organic vanilla extract

Instructions:

1. Preheat the oven to 350 degrees F.
2. Line a 9-inch greased springform with a piece of foil.
3. For crust: in a bowl, add all ingredients and mix until a crumbly mixture is formed.
4. Place the crust into the bottom of prepared pan, pressing in the bottom and a little up the sides.
5. Bake for about 10-12 minutes.
6. Remove from the oven and set aside onto a wire rack to cool for at least 10 minutes.
7. For filling: in a large bowl, add the cream cheese and Erythritol and beat until fluffy.
8. Add 1 egg at a time and with a wire whisk, beat until well combined after each addition.
9. Add the lemon juice and vanilla extract and beat until well combined.
10. Place the filling over the crust evenly and with the back of a spatula, smooth the top surface.
11. Bake for about 45-55 minutes.
12. Remove from the oven and set aside onto a wire rack to cool completely.
13. Refrigerate for about 4 hours.
14. Cut into desired sized slices and serve.

Nutritional Information per Serving:

Calories: 331
Fat: 31.2g
Sat Fat: 15.7g
Carbohydrates: 4.7g
Fiber: 1.5g
Sugar: 0.3g
Protein: 8.5g
Sodium: 213mg

Strawberry Cheesecake

Yield: 8 servings
Preparation Time: 20 minutes

Ingredients:

For Crust:

- ¾ cup unsweetened coconut, shredded
- ¾ cup raw sunflower seeds
- ¼ cup Erythritol
- ¼ teaspoon salt
- 3 tablespoons butter, melted

For Filling:

- 2 cups fresh strawberries, hulled and sliced
- 1½ teaspoons fresh lemon juice
- 1 teaspoon liquid stevia

- ¼ teaspoon salt
- 8-ounce cream cheese softened
- ½ teaspoon organic vanilla extract
- 1 cup heavy cream

Instructions:

1. For crust: place all the ingredients except butter in a food processor and pulse until a fine crumb mixture forms.
2. While motor is running, add butter and pulse until well combined.
3. Now, palace the mixture into a 9-inch pie dish and with your hands, press the mixture in the bottom and up sides.
4. With a paper towel wipe out the blender.
5. Now in a blender, add strawberries, lemon juice, stevia, and salt and pulse until puree forms.
6. Transfer the puree into a bowl.
7. In a bowl, add cream cheese and beat until smooth.
8. Add vanilla extract and heavy cream and beat until fluffy.
9. Add puree mixture and mix until well combined.
10. Place the strawberry mixture over crust mixture and freeze for at least 4-8 hours.
11. Cut in 8 equal sized slices and serve.

Nutritional Information per Serving:

Calories: 254
Fat: 24.6g
Sat Fat: 14.9g
Carbohydrates: 6g
Fiber: 1.8g
Sugar: 2.5g
Protein: 3.9g
Sodium: 197mg

Lime Pie

Yield: 8 servings
Preparation Time: 20 minutes
Cooking Time: 20 minutes

Ingredients:

For Crust:

- ½ cup almond flour
- ½ cup coconut flour sifted
- ¼ cup Erythritol
- ¼ cup butter, melted
- 2 organic eggs
- ¼ teaspoon salt

For Filling:

- ¾ cup unsweetened coconut milk
- ½ cup Erythritol
- ¼ cup heavy cream
- 2 teaspoons xanthan gum
- 1 teaspoon guar gum
- ¼ teaspoon powdered stevia
- 3 organic egg yolks

- ½ cup key lime juice
- 2 tablespoons unsweetened dried coconut

For Topping:

- 1 cup whipped cream
- ½ lemon, cut into slices

Instructions:

1. Preheat the oven to 400 degrees F.
2. For crust: in a bowl, add all ingredients and mix until well combined.
3. With your hands, knead the dough for about 1 minute.
4. Make a ball from the dough.
5. Arrange the dough ball between 2 sheets of wax paper and roll into a 1/8-inch thick circle.
6. In a 9-inch pie dish, place the dough and with your hands, press the mixture in the bottom and up sides.
7. Now, with a fork, prick the bottom and sides of crust at many places.
8. Bake for about 10 minutes.
9. Remove from oven and place the crust onto a wire rack to cool.
10. Now, set the oven to 350 degrees F.
11. For filling: in a food processor, add coconut milk, Erythritol, heavy cream, xanthan gum, guar gum, and stevia and pulse until well combined.
12. Add egg yolks and lime juice and pulse until well combined.
13. Spread the filling mixture over crust evenly.
14. Bake for about 10 minutes.
15. Remove from oven and place onto the wire rack to cool for about 10 minutes.
16. Freeze for about 3-4 hours before serving.
17. Serve with the topping of whipped cream and lemon slices.

Nutritional Information per Serving:

Calories: 276
Fat: 24.4g
Sat Fat: 14.2g
Carbohydrates: 9.6g
Fiber: 4.8g
Sugar: 1g
Protein: 5.9g
Sodium: 157mg

Blueberry Cobbler

Yield: 10 servings
Preparation Time: 15 minutes
Cooking Time: 22 minutes

Ingredients:

For Filling:

- 3 cups fresh blueberries
- 2 tablespoons Erythritol
- ¼ teaspoon xanthan gum

- 1 teaspoon fresh lemon juice

For Topping:

- 2/3 cup almond flour
- 2 tablespoons Erythritol
- 2 tablespoons butter, melted
- ½ teaspoon fresh lemon zest, grated finely

Instructions:

1. Preheat the oven to 375 degrees F.
2. For filling: in a bowl, add all ingredients and mix well.
3. Transfer the mixture into a 9x9-inch pie dish and with the back of the spoon, press to smooth the surface.
4. For topping: in a bowl, add all ingredients and mix until a crumbly mixture forms.
5. Place the crumble mixture over blueberry mixture evenly.
6. Bake for about 22 minutes or until top becomes golden brown.
7. Serve warm.

Nutritional Information per Serving:

Calories: 88
Fat: 6.2g
Sat Fat: 1.6g
Carbohydrates: 8g
Fiber: 1.9g
Sugar: 4.6g
Protein: 2g
Sodium: 18mg

Strawberry & Rhubarb Crumble

Yield: 8 servings
Preparation Time: 20minutes
Cooking Time: 35 minutes

Ingredients:

For Crumb:

- 1 cup rhubarb, chopped finely
- 1 cup fresh strawberries, hulled and chopped finely
- 1 tablespoon fresh lemon juice
- 1 teaspoon stevia & Erythritol blend
- ½ teaspoon xanthan gum

For Topping:

- 1 cup walnuts, chopped finely
- ½ cup coconut flour

- ¼ cup flaxseed meal
- ¼ cup plus 1 teaspoon stevia & Erythritol blend
- ¼ teaspoon sea salt
- 6 tablespoons unsalted butter, melted

Instructions:

1. Preheat the oven to 350 degrees F.
2. Grease a 9-inch pie dish.
3. For filling: in a bowl, add all ingredients and toss to combine well.
4. For topping: in another bowl, add walnuts, flour, flaxseed meal, ¼ cup of stevia blend and salt and mix until well combined.
5. Add butter and mix until a crumbly mixture is formed.
6. Transfer about ½ cup of the crumb mixture in a small bowl and stir in the remaining stevia blend.
7. Now, place the crumb mixture into the prepared pie dish and with the back of the spoon, press to smooth in the bottom evenly.
8. Place the filling mixture over the crust evenly and top with the remaining crumb mixture.
9. With a piece of foil, cover the baking dish and bake for about 20 minutes.
10. Remove the piece of foil and bake for about 10-15 minutes more.
11. Remove from the oven and set aside to cool slightly.
12. Serve warm.

Nutritional Information per Serving:

Calories: 233
Fat: 19.8g
Sat Fat: 6.7g
Carbohydrates: 10g
Fiber: 6g
Sugar: 1.3g
Protein: 5.8g
Sodium: 131mg

Chocolate Tart

Yield: 8 servings
Preparation Time: 20 minutes
Cooking Time: 5 minutes

Ingredients:

For Crust:

- 1¼ cups almond flour
- ¼ cup powdered Erythritol
- ¼ cup cacao powder
- 5 tablespoons butter, melted

For Filling:

- ¾ cup unsweetened almond milk
- ¾ cup whipping cream
- ¼ cup butter
- 1/3 cup powdered Erythritol
- 3-ounce 70% dark chocolate, chopped
- 3 tablespoons cacao powder
- ½ teaspoon espresso powder

- 3 large organic eggs

For Topping:

- 1 cup whipping cream
- 2 tablespoons powdered Erythritol
- ¼ teaspoon organic vanilla extract
- ½-ounce 70% dark chocolate shaving

Instructions:

1. For crust: lightly grease a 9-inch tart pan with a removable bottom.
2. In a bowl, add all ingredients and mix until well combined.
3. Place the crust the mixture into the prepared tart pan and with your hands, press the mixture in the bottom and up sides.
4. Refrigerate until using.
5. For filling: in a small pan, add almond milk, cream, and butter and bring to a boil.
6. Immediately, remove from heat.
7. In a blender, add Erythritol, chocolate, cacao powder, and espresso powder and pulse until well combined.
8. Add cream mixture and pulse until smooth.
9. Add eggs and pulse until smooth.
10. Place the filling mixture over crust evenly and refrigerate for about 2 hours.
11. Gently and carefully, press the tart pan from the bottom to remove the sides.
12. Transfer the tart onto a platter.
13. For topping: in a bowl, add whipping cream, Erythritol and vanilla extract and beat stiff peaks form.
14. Spread the cream mixture over filling evenly and garnish with chocolate shaving.
15. Refrigerate for about 15-20 minutes before serving.

Nutritional Information per Serving:

Calories: 421
Fat: 39.1g
Sat Fat: 19.2g
Carbohydrates: 10.1g
Fiber: 4.9g
Sugar: 0.2g
Protein: 9.5g
Sodium: 155mg

Mascarpone Tartlets

Yield: 12 servings
Preparation Time: 20 minutes
Cooking Time: 10 minutes

Ingredients:

For Crust:

- 2¼ cups almond flour
- ¼ cup powdered Swerve
- 5 tablespoons butter, melted
- ¼ teaspoon sea salt

For Mascarpone Cream:

- 6-ounces mascarpone cheese softened
- 2 tablespoons powdered Erythritol
- 1/3 cup heavy cream

- ¼ teaspoon fresh lemon zest, grated
- 1 teaspoon organic vanilla extract

For Garnishing:

- ¼ cup fresh strawberries, hulled and sliced
- ¼ cup fresh blueberries

Instructions:

1. Preheat the oven to 350 degrees F.
2. Grease 6 (4-inch) tart pans.
3. For crust: in a bowl, add all ingredients and mix until well combined.
4. Place the dough into prepared tart pans evenly and with your hands, press the mixture in the bottom and up sides.
5. With a fork, prick the bottom of all crusts.
6. Bake for about 8-10 minutes.
7. Remove from the oven and place onto wire rack to cool completely.
8. For the mascarpone cream: in a bowl, add mascarpone cheese and Erythritol and with a mixer, mix on low speed for about 2 minutes.
9. Slowly, add the heavy cream, beating continuously on low speed until well combined.
10. Now, beat on high speed for about 30-60 seconds or until thick.
11. Add the lemon zest and vanilla extract and beat until well combined.
12. Transfer the mascarpone cream into a piping bag, fitted with a large star-shaped tip and fill the tartlets.
13. Garnish with berries and serve.

Nutritional Information per Serving:

Calories: 208
Fat: 17.9g
Sat Fat: 5.7g
Carbohydrates: 5.8g
Fiber: 2.4g
Sugar: 0.5g
Protein: 6.3g
Sodium: 94mg

38497281R00076

Made in the USA
Middletown, DE
08 March 2019